D1236242

SCIENCE Q&A

MACHINES

— Janice Parker —

Weigl Publishers Inc.

Published by Weigl Publishers Inc.
350 5th Avenue, Suite 3304, PMB 6G
New York, NY 10118-0069

Website: www.weigl.com
Copyright ©2009 WEIGL PUBLISHERS INC.

All rights reserved. No part of this publication may be reproduced, stored in a retrieval system, or transmitted in any form or by any means, electronic, mechanical, photocopying, recording, or otherwise, without the prior written permission of the publisher.

All of the Internet URLs given in the book were valid at the time of publication. However, due to the dynamic nature of the Internet, some addresses may have changed, or sites may have ceased to exist since publication. While the author and publisher regret any inconvenience this may cause readers, no responsibility for any such changes can be accepted by either the author or the publisher.

Library of Congress Cataloging-in-Publication Data

Parker, Janice.
 Machines : Science Q & A / Janice Parker.
     p. cm.
 Includes index.
 ISBN 978-1-59036-950-0 (hard cover : alk. paper) -- ISBN 978-1-59036-951-7 (soft cover : alk. paper)
 1. Machinery--Juvenile literature. I. Title.
 TJ147.P34 2008
 621.8--dc22

                                2008003890

Printed in China
1 2 3 4 5 6 7 8 9 0 12 11 10 09 08

Project Coordinator
Heather Hudak

Design
Terry Paulhus

Photo credits
All images provided by Getty Images.

Every reasonable effort has been made to trace ownership and to obtain permission to reprint copyright material. The publishers would be pleased to have any errors or omissions brought to their attention so that they may be corrected in subsequent printings.

CONTENTS

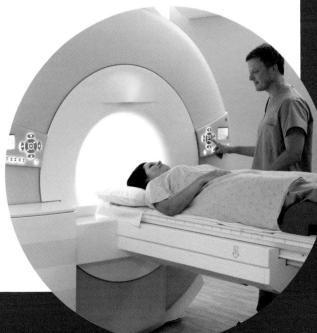

What are machines?

People rely on all types of machines to make life easier and more enjoyable. Our homes contain machines to wash and dry clothes, machines to keep and cook food, machines for communication, and machines for entertainment.

Machines help people work faster and more effectively. They move people from one place to another. Without machines, hospitals and clinics would not be able to treat many illnesses.

Many machines that help people were invented in the past one hundred years. Most of us use them every day without knowing how they work. We usually only think about these machines when they stop working and need to be repaired. Today, it is difficult to imagine living without all of the helpful machines we use.

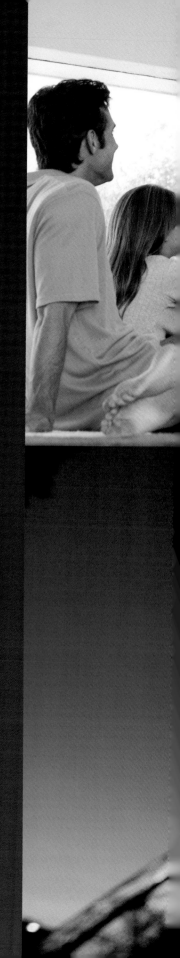

How do machines help people at home?

Many machines make people's home lives easier. Gas and electric ovens cook food with heat. The heat cooks the outside of the food first and then moves inward. Microwave ovens are much smaller, and they cook food more quickly than other ovens.

Microwave ovens use radiation, high-energy particles or rays, to cook food. Microwaves are electromagnetic waves, electrical and magnetic vibrations that travel through the air. Microwaves enter food and heat it evenly. As the microwave rays move through the food, they hit water, as well as sugar, fat, and salt molecules, and make them flip back and forth rapidly. The flip-flopping molecules rub against other molecules in the food. This rubbing together produces the energy that heats the food.

Radiation can be dangerous to human health. Microwave ovens have thick walls to prevent radiation from escaping the oven. They use much less electricity to heat food than other types of ovens. This makes microwave ovens less harmful to the environment.

How does a microwave cook food?

Microwaves "bounce" off the inside walls of a microwave oven and penetrate the outer surface of the food.

The microwaves cause water molecules inside the food to move and bounce off each other, creating heat. This heat spreads into the center of the food to cook it.

Wave of the future

Microwave ovens were invented by physicist Percy Le Baron Spencer in 1946. He discovered that microwaves could be used to cook food after high-**frequency** radio waves melted a bar of chocolate in his pocket.

How do refrigerators keep food cold?

Refrigerators keep food at a constant cool temperature. Without these machines, we would not be able to keep food fresh for several days at a time. Refrigerators prevent food from becoming dangerous to eat by slowing the growth of microbes, or disease-causing bacteria.

To keep cool, refrigerators use a chemical called a coolant. The coolant moves in a cycle through small pipes contained within the walls of the refrigerator. As the coolant moves through the pipes, it changes from a liquid to a gas and back to a liquid again. When a liquid vaporizes, or changes into a gas, it absorbs heat from its surroundings. This cools off the air and nearby objects. Coolant near the inside of the refrigerator vaporizes, cooling down the air and food inside.

■ Old refrigerators that contain harmful chemicals must be disposed of in specific ways to help the environment. Fridges can also be recycled.

As the coolant continues through its cycle, it begins to heat up again. When a gas turns into a liquid, it heats up the surrounding area. This is why the coolant pipes near the outside walls of the refrigerator feel hot.

Here is your challenge!

On a piece of paper, make two columns. In the first column, list all the machines that you think you use often.

For one week, put a check mark in the second column each time you use a particular machine. Make sure to add items that are not already on your list.

At the end of the week, add up the check marks to see which machines you use the most. Try to imagine what your life would be like without these machines. Circle the machines that are most important to you.

How do digital cameras work?

When you take a picture with a camera, the camera records the image as a photograph. Photographs allow us to see a specific moment in time, long after the moment has passed.

22.jpg

clouds 23.jpg

7.8-23.4mm 1:2.8-4.9

find it quick

To learn more about digital cameras, visit **http://electronics.howstuffworks.com/ digital-camera.htm**.

Light rays enter a camera through its lens. The reflected light from an object is translated into computer language by a computer inside the camera. The computer language is a series of "0"s and "1"s that are used to represent different colored dots. The picture is made up of thousands, or even millions, of colored dots called pixels.

Before a picture is taken, a camera must focus on the subject. To focus, the camera lens is adjusted until the image appears clear. Some cameras must be focused by hand, while others automatically adjust.

Next, the exposure must be chosen. The exposure is how much time passes when the photo is being taken. The exposure

■ Digital cameras have a screen on the back. This allows the photographer to see the image even before the picture is taken.

time depends on how much light enters the camera and the shutter speed. The shutter lets light in through the lens. Exposure time is usually a fraction of a second. Many cameras focus and set the exposure time automatically.

When the picture has been recorded in the camera, the user can transfer it to their computer and print it. Most digital cameras use a removable storage device, such as a memory card. This device holds the pictures and can be transferred from the camera to a computer. A computer can be used to share pictures online or to print them on photographic paper.

Picture perfect

Digital cameras allow the user to see the image seconds after taking the picture. If the user does not like the image, he or she can delete it and try again.

How do video games work?

Video game systems, or consoles, have become a very common part of homes in many parts of the world. These devices were only invented in the 1970s and have gone through many changes over the years. Today's video games feature realistic graphics and interactive gameplay.

Game consoles are similar to home computers. These computers are built to perform a number of functions, such as word processing, surfing the Internet, and gaming. Consoles are designed for only one function—gaming. This means that all of the console's parts are designed for a better gaming experience.

■ Today, video games include wireless remote controls that simulate real tools and instruments, for more realistic gameplay.

The most important aspect of a video game is the ability of the user to interact with the game system. This means that, when the user pushes a button or moves a thumbstick, the game responds by changing to the next screen or by moving the character. This is controlled by something called the user control interface. Without this component, video games would not exist.

Game consoles are easy to set up and use. They easily become a part of a home entertainment system. They connect to the television and stereo, and can even connect to other consoles through the Internet. This means that users can play online with people all over the world.

Name of the game

In 1889, the Marufuku Company was founded in Japan, making playing cards. The company changed its name in 1951 to The Nintendo Playing Card Company. Today, Nintendo is one of the world's most well known video game companies. Nintendo is a Japanese word meaning "leave luck to heaven."

Nintendo®

How do machines keep people safe?

Many special machines help keep our homes and other buildings safe. Some of these machines are simple devices, such as door locks, while others are quite complex. Many homes and office buildings have security systems to help protect the people and objects inside.

Security systems use electronic sensors, devices that react to light, motion, and heat, to gather information about a building. If someone tries to break into a building, sensors detect the movement and send a message to the alarm system. The alarm system alerts the police or a security company.

There are several types of sensors used for security systems. Vibration sensors are placed on windows. These sensors detect any movement of the glass. If the glass is broken, sensors set off an alarm. Magnetic sensors are often used on doors. One magnet is attached to the door, and a second is attached to the door frame. The two magnets are connected when the door is shut. If the door is opened, the magnetic connection is broken, sending a signal to the alarm system. **Infrared** sensors, made up of light we cannot see, can sense the heat created by a human body. If a person enters an area where there are supposed to be no people, the alarm sounds.

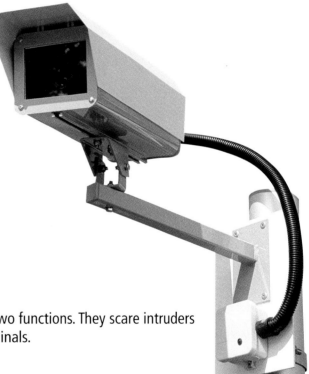

■ Security cameras serve two functions. They scare intruders away and help identify criminals.

Cause for alarm

Smoke detectors save lives by alerting people to fires in their home or office. Some alarms contain a light source and a light-sensitive device called a photocell. Smoke scatters light from the source and reflects onto the photocell. This sets the alarm off.

How do machines help people work?

Most workplaces use machines to help people do different tasks.

Office machines may include anything from coffeemakers to calculators to robots that perform tasks people used to do. Machines in the workplace allow people to work more efficiently and more quickly. Companies rely on machines to make products quickly and cheaply.

New technology means that the workplace is constantly changing. Workers must keep up with these changes by learning about new machines or computer programs. Some people argue that machines do too much work that could be done by people. Most people agree that machines help make the workplace more efficient by doing jobs that people cannot do or do not like to do. Robots and computers are often used to carry out tasks that are too difficult or too dangerous for people to carry out.

■ Machines allow workers to easily lift and move objects that weigh thousands of pounds.

One layer at a time

Color photocopiers use only black and three colors—blue, red, and yellow—to copy any color picture. **Filters** break down the original picture into the three different colors of light. By applying separate layers of black and of each color, the copier can duplicate any color.

How do metal detectors work?

Security gates at airports and other buildings prevent people from carrying guns, knives, and other weapons into the building or onto an airplane.

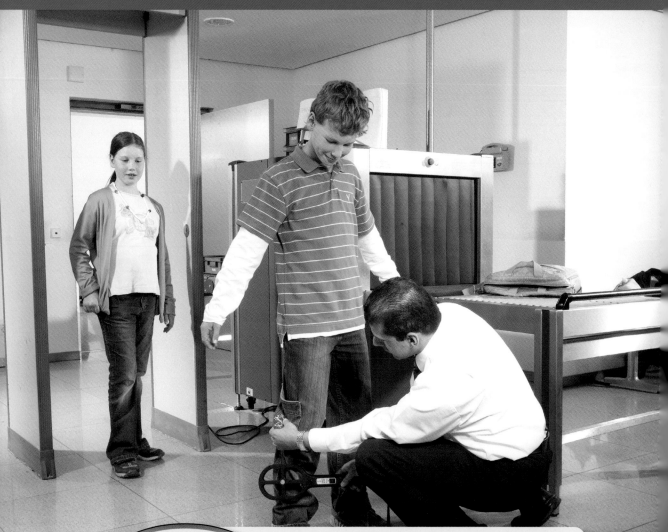

find it quick

Learn more about how metal detectors and other machines are used to keep airports and air travel safe. Visit **http://travel.howstuff works.com/airport-security.htm**.

A

If a person carrying a weapon made of metal walks through a metal detector, an alarm sounds, alerting security.

Simple transmission devices are made up of wire coils, creating a magnetic field. When someone walks through the field with a piece of metal, the metal creates another magnetic field. This field reverses the flow of electricity in the first field. A message is sent to the detector indicating that metal is present. Then, the machine's alarms sound.

Security guards check the person to see what might have set off the alarm. Guards can adjust the gate to sound the alarm if someone is only carrying a large amount of metal. Often, the coils in the gates are designed to sense any metal. Even a few coins in a pocket or the zipper on a jacket can set off an alarm.

■ Land mines are explosives that are placed underground. They explode when a person steps on or drives over them. Metal detectors are used to find land mines so they can be removed.

Buried treasure

Handheld metal detectors can be used to find metal buried underground. These detectors create a small magnetic field. The detector is slowly moved over the ground. An alarm sounds when the magnetic field comes into contact with certain types of metal.

How does an elevator work?

Most buildings that are taller than three stories have elevators that move people and heavy objects to different floors. Elevators are boxes that move up and down on strong metal cables along elevator shafts, or well-like narrow spaces. Some elevators can travel to hundreds of different floors.

find it quick

Believe it or not, there are people trying to build elevators to space. To learn more about the space elevator, log on to **www.pbs.org/wgbh/nova/sciencenow/3401/02.html**.

A pulley uses a wheel to support or guide a cable riding in a groove in its edge. Many elevators use a pulley system that is powered by an electric motor. Counterweights, or heavy objects that move in the opposite direction of the elevator, help move the elevator box up and down more easily. The counterweights reduce the power that is needed to operate the elevator.

Passengers enter the elevator and press a button. An electric signal is sent from the button to the elevator control box. The control box tells the elevator which direction and floor the passenger has chosen. The pulley system then takes the elevator box to the correct floor.

■ Elevators at some landmarks, such as the Skylon at Niagara Falls, are on the outside of the building. This allows passengers to enjoy the view while they travel up and down.

Safe and sound

Most elevators have safety features to protect passengers if the machine breaks down. If a cable breaks, these elevators have teeth that clamp onto the shaft so the box will not fall.

What do generators do?

Generators are machines that convert one form of energy into another kind of energy. They allow other machines to work. Electrical generators convert energy into electricity that can power lamps, household appliances, and other devices.

find it quick

Learn about turning water into electricity by visiting **www.eia.doe.gov/kids/energyfacts**.

Power plants use large generators to produce electricity. Small, portable generators are useful during blackouts and in remote places where there is no access to power plants.

The first electrical generator was built by a scientist named Michael Faraday in 1831. Faraday discovered that, when a coil of wire moves near a magnet, an electrical current is created. When the magnet moves in one direction, current flows in one direction. When

■ Dams use generators to turn the power of water into electricity. These are called hydroelectric generators.

the magnet moves in the other direction, near the coil, the current in the wire flows in the opposite direction.

By moving the coil and the magnet back and forth, a continuous electric current is produced. Faraday made a device that had a rotating coil attached to a magnet. Other scientists have since improved this design.

Harness the wind

One very old type of generator is a windmill. The first windmills were built around 1,500 years ago. They were used to pump water. Windmills use wind power to turn the blades or sails. Today, windmills can be used to generate electricity.

How is remote control used?

Many machines are not automatic—they need to be controlled by people. Sometimes, machines need to be controlled by people standing a long way away.

Remote control allows people to operate a machine from a distance. The operator of the machine uses a control box to change the movements of the machine. The control box sends messages to the machine either through long wires or radio waves.

Most people use remote control every day in their homes when they watch television. When a button is pressed on a television remote control, the information is sent to the television by infrared light signals. Infrared light cannot be seen by the human eye. The television sensor picks up the infrared message, and the television makes the requested changes.

Remote control can also be used in situations that are dangerous to humans. It allows a person to control a machine without being in a dangerous area, such as near a bomb or deep under the sea.

■ The military use remote-controlled airplanes called drones. Pilots control these planes from the ground. Drones are able to perform many functions that normal military airplanes can, without endangering the pilot.

Robo cop

Robots are used by police to pick up objects that may be bombs. The robots are operated by remote control, so officers do not have to handle dangerous packages.

How do robots take jobs away from people?

Computers and robots are used more and more in the workplace. These machines can be very helpful. They can work 24 hours a day. They can also work in dangerous environments.

find it quick

To create your own robot, log on to **www.channel4.com/science/microsites/R/robots/constructor.html**, and play Robot Constructor.

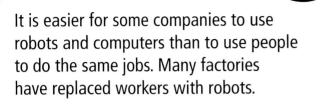

It is easier for some companies to use robots and computers than to use people to do the same jobs. Many factories have replaced workers with robots.

Some people believe that we rely too much on these new machines. They believe that some of these machines cannot do certain jobs as well as people can. Another worry is that these new technologies will put many more people out of work.

Other people think we should use machines at work whenever we can. To them, machines make our lives easier and give us more free time. They believe that people who lose their jobs due to robots and computers can train in other fields and start new careers.

■ In recent years, some companies have developed robots that can walk and talk.

Life on Mars

Robots have been sent to other planets, including Mars, to collect soil samples and take photographs. The information is sent back to scientists on Earth.

How do computers help people work faster?

Computers have changed the way most people work. They can perform many tasks, such as addition and multiplication of numbers, faster than a person can. Computers can also help us create graphs and images much more quickly than we could draw them by hand.

The "brain" of a computer is its microprocessor. The microprocessor is the **circuit** that allows a computer to perform all of its tasks. In addition to working with numbers, the microprocessor can move information from one area in the computer's memory to another. It can also be programmed to make decisions depending on what the computer user has typed into the computer.

■ Computers can be used for work or play. Many programs are both fun and educational.

The hard disk is the part of a computer that stores all of its information. A hard disk works much the same way as a videocassette. It stores information as magnetic signals. Unlike a videocassette, a hard disk can store a huge amount of data.

Micro machine

The first microprocessor, the Intel 4004, was invented in 1971. It could add and subtract but was only able to work on four bits, or tiny pieces of information, at a time. Most of today's microprocessors work on 64 bits.

How do machines move people?

Over the years, people have used many different machines to get from one place to another. These machines can rely on simple or highly complex technology.

■ Steam trains were important machines in the past. They helped people reach faraway places in a short amount of time. This helped settlers move across the United States.

Bicycles are basic machines that provide a popular method of transportation. The invention of the steam engine meant that trains could transport people and goods quickly and farther away than horses and wagons could.

Modern machines, such as automobiles and airplanes, have changed the way people view the world. These modern methods of transportation allow people to travel quickly across the country and around the globe. Modern machines can even be used to travel to space.

Most modern vehicles are powered by engines. These engines need fuel to work. As the fuels are burned, they pollute the environment. Engineers are trying to create new vehicles that are less damaging to Earth.

Here is your challenge!

You can make a steamboat using a small metal tube, paper clips, a candle, and water.

First, attach the metal tube to the top of a small toy boat. The open end of the tube should face the back of the boat. Fill the tube with water. Then, with an adult's help, place a candle on the boat, under the tube. Light the candle.

The flame from the candle will heat the water inside the tube. This will turn the water into steam, which escapes through the open end of the tube. The steam escaping from the tube will push your boat forward through the water.

What is the difference between a gasoline engine and a diesel engine?

Most vehicles use either gasoline or diesel, a type of light oil, as fuel for their engines.

Gasoline engines are the most common engines. They are a type of **internal combustion** engine. Fuel is burned in cylinders inside the engine. Cylinders are hollow metal tubes with circular walls.

There are two ways in which fuel is brought to a gas engine. In vehicles with carburetion systems, a device called a carburetor mixes air and gasoline. This mixture is sucked into the cylinders in the engine. Spark plugs ignite the mixture, causing small explosions. These explosions create hot gases that force down a piston, which is a cylinder-shaped plug that moves snugly up and down inside the cylinder. The movement of the pistons moves another device, called the crankshaft, which in turn moves the wheels of the vehicle. In fuel-injected engines, which are found in most newer cars, the fuel is automatically put into each cylinder in the engine. Most gas engines use port fuel injection. This means the fuel is injected just above the intake valves of the cylinders.

■ Automobile companies have developed diesel engines that are more efficient and less damaging to the environment.

Diesel engines work the same way as gas engines, except they do not need spark plugs. The fuel explosions are caused by heat and pressure created when diesel fuel is pressed into the cylinders. A diesel engine uses direct fuel injection.

Full steam ahead

The steam engine is an example of an external combustion engine. Internal combustion engines must use a pure liquid oil or gas fuel to run. Steam engines can use anything that burns as fuel, such as coal, wood, or even newspaper.

What is a jet engine?

Airplanes have powerful engines to keep them in the air. Most large airplanes have jet engines.

Jet engines, also called gas **turbine** engines, send hot air out the back of the airplane. This force moves the airplane forward. The jet engine burns jet fuel. The burning fuel heats up the air and makes it expand. This expanded, or pressurized, air then rushes out of the back of the engine. The air turns the turbine in the engine.

The front of a jet engine has an area to collect and compress, or squeeze, the incoming air. The air helps burn fuel. The burning fuel and air make a high-pressure gas, which is sent to the

■ Air Force fighter jets use jet engines. These planes can fly faster than 1,000 miles (1,609 km) per hour.

turbine. The movement of the gas makes the blades of the turbine spin, powering the airplane.

Very large jet planes use turbofan engines. These are the same as other gas turbine engines, except they have large fans at the front. These fans help bring even more air into the engine. A turboprop engine is similar to a turbofan engine, but it has a propeller at the front of the engine instead of fans.

Big air

The Airbus A380 is the world's largest commercial airplane. It can hold up to 853 passengers. The A380 is 240 feet (73 meters) long and 79 feet (24 m) high. Its wingspan is 262 feet (80 m).

How do machines hurt the environment?

While machines help people work and live more easily, they can have a negative impact on the environment.

find it quick

Visit **www.epa.gov/acidrain/index.html** to learn more about what causes acid rain and what is being done to stop it.

■ Automobiles are required to have emission control devices. These devices lessen the amount of harmful chemicals that are released from automobile engines.

Acid rain is the term used to describe rain, snow, or other wet precipitation that has been **contaminated** by pollution. It is caused by high levels of certain chemicals in the air. These chemicals fall down to Earth with rain. Acid rain can harm plants and animals by damaging the places they live and the food they eat. It can also damage buildings.

The main causes of acid rain are chemicals released into the air by machines. Factories that send harmful gases, such as sulfur dioxide and nitrogen oxide, into the air are the biggest sources of acid rain. Automobile engines are some of the worst offenders. They give off harmful gases in their **emissions** when they burn gasoline.

Here is your challenge!

Many historical buildings and statues are made of limestone, the same material used to make chalk. This material is easily damaged by acid rain.

Place a piece of chalk in a bowl. Slowly pour vinegar over the chalk. Vinegar is an acid. What happens to the chalk?

Write your observations in your notebook. Discuss the issue of acid rain with your friends and teacher.

What impact do cars have on the environment?

One of the problems with most methods of transportation is that they release chemicals into the environment. Vehicles that use engines release emissions into the air that can lead to acid rain and other types of pollution. Automobiles use **fossil fuels** such as oil and natural gas. There are limited amounts of fossil fuels on Earth.

Charging Battery

START

STOP

Battery Unit

Battery Control Unit

Battery Unit

Batt

find it quick

Find out more about alternative fuel systems at **www.energyquest.ca. gov/transportation/index.html**.

For many years, engineers have tried to create vehicles that do not pollute. In just a few years, many people may be driving electric vehicles, sometimes called EVs. EVs have engines that run on electricity instead of gasoline or diesel. Since they do not burn fuel, EVs do not release harmful emissions into the air. Some people do not believe that EVs are much better for the environment than automobiles that run on gasoline. This is because the generators that produce electricity to run EVs also pollute the environment.

Other cars are being designed to run on fuel cells that are powered by hydrogen, a gas. Hydrogen cars are considered to be the best for the environment. Instead of releasing dangerous emissions, hydrogen-powered cars only release water.

■ New engines have been developed that can burn either gasoline or hydrogen. When hydrogen is burned, the only emission is water vapor.

Sugar rush

Scientists have tried to use all types of substances, including sugar, to power cars. Sugar can be used to make a chemical called ethanol. When mixed with gasoline, ethanol creates fewer harmful emissions and uses less fossil fuel.

How do machines keep people healthy?

In the last century, medicine has gone through many changes. We can now help cure diseases and save lives by using machines.

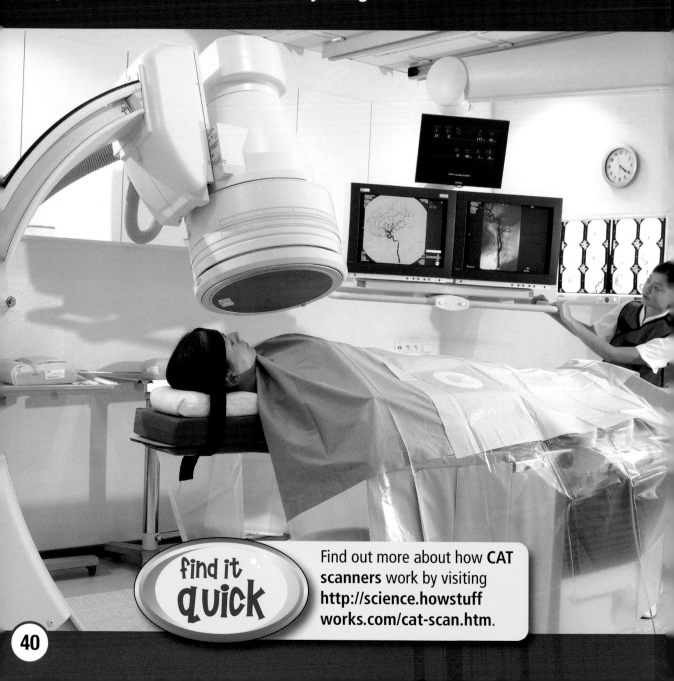

find it quick

Find out more about how **CAT scanners** work by visiting **http://science.howstuff works.com/cat-scan.htm**.

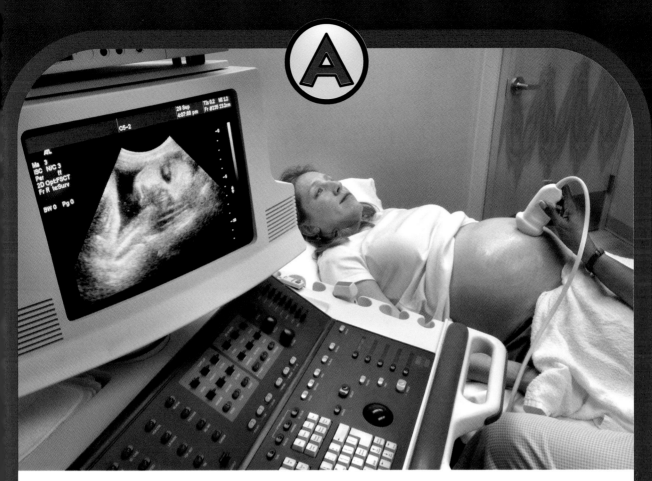

Machines are used in all areas of medicine. They help doctors quickly diagnose, or determine, the cause of health problems. Machines are also used in surgery and to help cure medical problems.

Basic machines, such as thermometers, have been used for many years. Newer machines, such as CAT scanners, are

■ Machines have made it possible to see babies even before they are born. Doctors can examine unborn babies for health issues.

being used more and more to help find health problems before they can harm people. Health care workers must know how to use modern medical equipment.

Mouthful

Before machines were available, doctors had to use different methods to help patients. In ancient Greece, doctors used their hand to measure a patient's body temperature. The mouth thermometer was not invented until the early 17th century, by an Italian named Santorio.

How do people take photographs of bones?

People often get injured but do not know exactly what is wrong with them. If you hurt your arm, you might think that it is broken but cannot be sure just by looking at it or feeling it. Usually, a person in this situation goes for an x-ray.

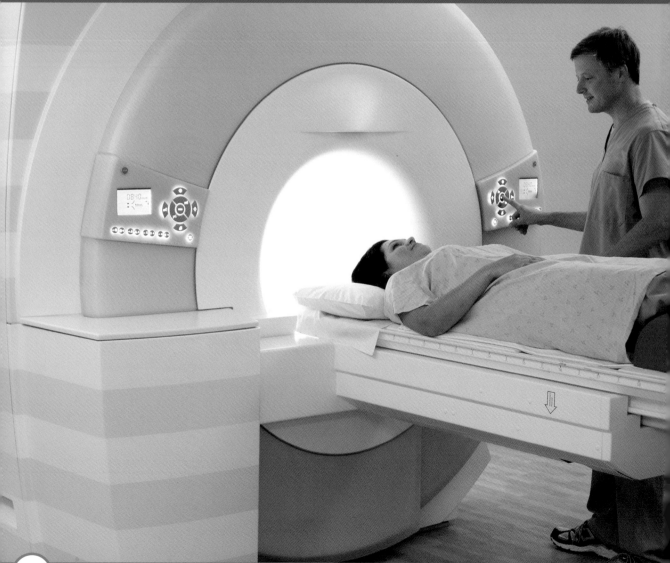

An x-ray travels through a person's skin and muscles to take a photograph of the bones inside the body. Using these photographs, doctors can see if bones are broken without having to open the body.

An x-ray is a type of invisible wave. X-rays move through the body and are absorbed only by dense material such as bone. An x-ray machine has a tube that makes the rays and directs them onto the human body. The rays that pass through the body cause changes in the film that allow it to be developed into a visible image. The final image is called a radiograph. Bones show up as light or white areas on a radiograph. Other body parts appear black.

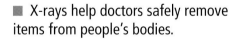 X-rays help doctors safely remove items from people's bodies.

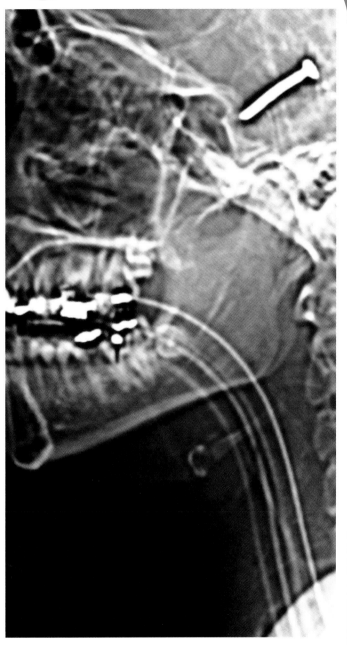

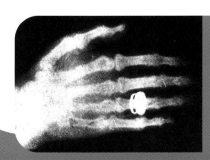

X-wife

Wilhelm Roentgen discovered x-rays in 1895. The first radiograph was an image of his wife's hand.

Careers with machines

Commercial Pilot

Commercial pilots fly airplanes for airline companies. They transport passengers, goods, or mail across the country or around the world. Most large passenger planes have two pilots—the captain and the copilot. Much of their work is done before the plane even leaves the ground.

Pilots check weather conditions and prepare a flight plan. They then board the plane and check emergency equipment, flight instruments, radios, fuel supply, landing gear, and other equipment.

In order to become a pilot, one must take special courses and spend many hours in flight training.

Ultrasound Technician

Ultrasound scanners give off ultrasonic waves, which are sounds that people cannot hear. These waves bounce off different parts inside the body and send back an echo. Ultrasound machines change the echoes into pictures, called **sonograms**.

Ultrasound machines create images of the shape and movement of blood, internal organs, and other body tissues. Ultrasound is often used to check the health of unborn babies and any unusual growths in the body. Ultrasound technologists work in hospitals or in medical clinics. They use ultrasound equipment to gain information about patients.

Most jobs today involve machines in some way. Visit **www.gettech.org/txt/ careers_txt.asp?category=1** to find out more about some of these jobs.

Young scientists at work
Test Your Knowledge

You can build a car out of a mousetrap. Mousetraps can be dangerous, so get help from an adult.

Materials:

1 mousetrap

2 small wooden or metal rods

4 eyehole screws

1 foam board

2 rubber bands

String

4 millimeter-diameter washers

Glue

Directions:

Screw two eyehole screws into each end of the mousetrap near the edges. Insert the wooden or metal rods through the eyehole screws. The rods will act as the axels of your car. Cut four large wheels out of the foam board. Find the exact center of each wheel and attach them to the ends of the rods.

Glue the rubber bands around the rear wheels. These will help the wheels grip the ground. Attach one end of the string to the metal arm on the trap. Wrap the other end of the string tightly around the rear axel. When you release the trap, the string will unravel from the axel and push the car forward.

Take a machines survey

Answer the questions about machines, and see how you compare to other Americans.

1. Do you have a telephone at home? How many phones do you have?

2. Do you own a radio? How many radios does your family have?

3. Is there a television at home? How many?

4. Do you own a video game console?

5. Do you have a computer at home? If not, do you use a computer at school or anywhere else?

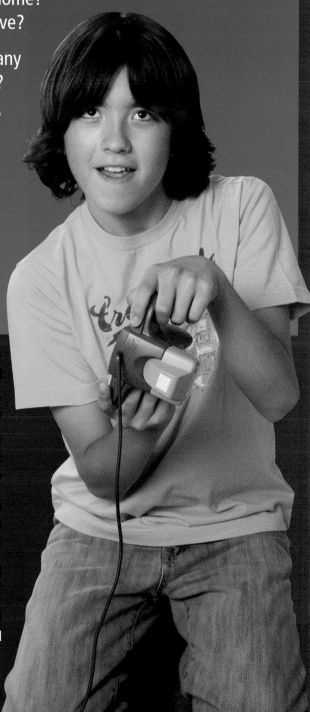

RESULTS: 1. Telephones can be found in 98 percent of American homes.

2. On average, every home in the United States has 5.6 radios.

3. The average American home has more than two televisions. In fact, there are more televisions than people in the United States.

4. Of the homes that have televisions, 41 percent also have a video game console. That is almost 46 million homes.

5. Of homes with children aged between six and 17, 76 percent have a computer. Eighty-six percent of American children between ages 3 and 17 use a computer at home, school, or work.

Fast Facts

Archimedes, a mathematician in ancient Greece, invented a machine called the Archimedean screw that can raise water from deep under the ground.

Computers contain tiny **silicon** chips. These chips have electrical circuits that can store enormous amounts of information.

The first electronic calculator was invented in 1963. It was as big as a cash register. Today, calculators can fit into a wristwatch.

Fax machines change words and images into electric signals that can be sent over telephone lines.

Sputnik I, the first **satellite**, was sent into orbit around Earth in 1957. Satellites are now used for space research, weather prediction, and communication.

Radar (Radio Detection and Ranging) was developed over a period of 40 years. During World War II, it helped airplanes and ships see other objects in the dark.

In 1976, the world's fastest commercial airplane, the Concorde, began carrying passengers. The Concorde flew at about 1,500 miles (2,410 km) per hour.

Many modern watches and clocks contain the mineral quartz. An electric current makes the quartz crystals vibrate at a constant rate.

The wheel is one of the simplest machines in the world. The oldest wheel found is from about 3500 BC.

The fastest trains in the world are powered by electricity. They can travel faster than 310 miles (500 km) per hour.

Glossary

CAT scanners: machines used to take images of the inside of the body

circuit: a path followed by electrical currents

contaminated: made dirty

emissions: gases that are released into the air by machines

filters: devices that clean or simplify substances

fossil fuels: fuels created millions of years ago from the remains of plants and animals

frequency: the number of times an electric wave vibrates each second

infrared: invisible light waves that can be felt as heat

internal combustion: when fuel burns inside an engine

satellite: a machine that orbits a planet or other object in space

silicon: an element used to make computer chips

sonograms: images of the inside of a person's body created by an ultrasound machine

turbine: a steam-, water-, or air-powered machine that has rotating blades

Index

DATE DUE

4/6/15			
APR 04 2016			
			PRINTED IN U.S.A.